FENG SHUI

DOs & TABOOs

ANGI MA WONG

STOREY BOOKS

The mission of Storey Publishing is to serve our customers by publishing practical information that encourages personal independence in harmony with the environment.

Edited by Deborah Balmuth, Karen Levy, and Jennifer Travis Donnelly
Cover design by Leslie Constantino
Text design by Erin Lincourt
Book layout by Susan Bernier

The information in this book is true and complete to the best of our knowledge. All recommendations are made without guarantee on the part of the author or Storey Publishing. The author and publisher disclaim any liability in connection with the use of this information. For additional information please contact Storey Publishing, 210 MASS MoCA Way, North Adams, MA 01247.

Storey books are available for special premium and promotional uses and for customized editions. For further information, please call 800-793-9396.

Printed in the United States by Command Web

20 19 18 17 16 15 14 13 12 11 10

Library of Congress Cataloging-in-Publication Data
Wong, Angi Ma.
    Feng Shui dos & taboos / Angi Ma Wong.
        p. cm.
    ISBN 1-58017-308-X (alk. paper)
    1. Feng-shui—Dictionaries. I. Title.

BF1779.F4 W65 2000
133.3'337--dc21   00-057346

CONTENTS

FOREWORD

Feng Shui is a fascinating subject that has been part of my life for almost half a century. I have personally seen fortunes rise and fall because of the application or misapplication of feng shui. It is an intricate process, requiring patience and years of careful experience. Simple improvements may require only obvious changes and customary placements of objects. However, the intricate formulas for positional, locational, and time-dimensional energies can change lives and are what fascinate and confound people worldwide.

Hectic schedules and limited time mean many people don't have the patience to study feng shui. Some find its complicated applications too overwhelming or too arduous. What people crave is a simplified version that can be implemented quickly and easily. That is what makes Angi Ma Wong's book so unique.

I had the good fortune of having Angi attend my class in Los Angeles. A talented, knowledgeable, and humble person, Angi has proved her potential once again in the pages of this book. I am honored to write the foreword and to see a former student doing so well. I congratulate her on her excellent work and hope it becomes a stepping stone for her readers.

One good feng shui tip is a precious jewel. This book is a virtual gold mine of nuggets that represent easy and effective changes in your life. May feng shui bring you as much success, fun, and good fortune as it has brought me.

YAP CHENG HAI, Co-Founder
Yap Cheng Hai Feng Shui Center of Excellence
http://www.ychfengshui.com

Recently, feng shui has captured the imagination of the media and has become trendy. I believe its global appeal and popularity coincide with the spiritual black hole in so many people's lives. In the past millennium, humankind's achievements have mostly focused on medicine, science, and technology. But for all the gadgets, inventions, and equipment that we use, it is a paradox that we work longer and harder than any generation before us. We spend so much of our time using machines that a great deal of our humanity has been lost.

Feng shui offers a return to a simpler, more intuitive, natural way of living that fulfills a deep need for many people. But it must be done in concert with your spiritual, emotional, and physical health. Practicing this ancient art while neglecting these other aspects of your life weakens its effectiveness. As you practice feng shui, be sure it is with a pure heart and in moderation. Keep a journal of the feng shui changes you implement and what happens after you do. Be patient, as there is a reason and a season for everything in our lives. And remember, feng shui is as much about symbolism as it is about placement.

This art has been an integral part of my Chinese upbringing and vital to my personal and professional life. I look forward to sharing it with you to help you achieve serenity, contentment, and peace of mind.

ANGI MA WONG

www.FengShuiLady.com
e-mail: amawong@worldnet.att.net

ACKNOWLEDGMENTS

My grateful appreciation and thanks go to
Master Yap Cheng Hai, Joey Yap,
Lillian Ng, Dixon Hsu, and Tina Wingerter
for their support of this book.

INTRODUCTION

INTRODUCTION

Throughout history, cultures around the world have believed that spirits dwelled in nature, the weather, and things they could not explain but intuitively sensed were special. Even primitive peoples identified natural places they considered unique and sacred. To the ancient Chinese, that feeling was captured in the philosophy of feng shui.

FENG SHUI PHILOSOPHY

Literally translated as "wind-water," feng shui is the art of placement and is one of the five components of a person's destiny. The first factor, fate, is determined by heaven at the moment of your birth. Luck, the second element, occurs in the form of pure luck, man-made luck, and heaven luck. The third component is feng shui, or earth luck. Next comes philanthropy, and finally education and experience.

I like the analogy that life is a journey from one place to another. You start out in a particular circumstance, but the choices and decisions you make determine your mode of transportation. The last three components of your destiny are the proactive things you can do to make changes along the way.

FENG SHUI CONCEPTS

The three major concepts of feng shui are **the flow of energy; the balance of yin and yang; and the interaction of the five elements in the**

universe: fire, earth, metal, water, and wood. The flow of energy is expressed in nature, where perfectly straight lines occur only in very short segments, such as sugar cane and bamboo stalks. Even the tallest trees have irregularities, and it is a natural law that energy flows in wavy lines similar to breezes and streams. When energy travels in a straight path, as in the case of a roaring flood, its awesome power is unleashed. When a flood destroys everything in its path, it usually follows something man-made, such as a road. Freeways, tunnels, bridges, buildings, and lampposts have straight edges that are conduits of negative energy called *sha* or "killing" energy. In feng shui, straight lines and the angles they create are called "killing" arrows.

The second important concept is the duality of the universe, expressed in the yin/yang symbol of one dark and one light teardrop positioned in a circle. One teardrop embodies yin qualities, which are female, soft, passive, nurturing, dark, fluid, even numbers, and the right side of the body. The other teardrop signifies yang traits, which are male, bright, hard, active, aggressive, odd numbers, and the left side of the body. The two halves comprise a whole, yet there is an element of each in the other.

yin/yang symbol

A fluid S-shaped line divides the two teardrops and personifies the balance within the universe, nature, the environment, and the self. It is our task to maintain the balance of yin and yang within our physical, mental, emotional, spiritual, and intellectual selves. Achieving this balance results in feeling grounded — much like a rock that is pounded by the elements but remains solid.

The third concept includes the five universal elements, each of which relates to the others in two ways: a generative or creative connection that provides strength and power, and an overpowering or destructive relationship that denies strength and power. Knowledge of these relationships is critical in feng shui; placement based on misinformation or ignorance can result in an effect opposite to the one you want to achieve.

GENERATIVE CYCLE

Fire generates earth
Earth generates metal
Metal generates water
Water generates wood
Wood generates fire

DESTRUCTIVE CYCLE

Fire melts metal
Metal cuts wood
Wood moves earth
Earth dams water
Water puts out fire

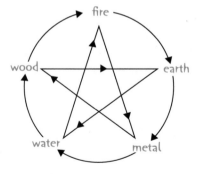

INTRODUCTION

SCHOOLS OF THOUGHT

Two of the most popular forms of feng shui are the Compass School and the Black (Hat) Sect Tantric Tibetan Buddhist (BSTB) School. For thousands of years, the Compass School has been recognized as the traditional, classic feng shui practice; it uses either a Chinese or a Western-style compass to determine the exact direction of the main entrance to a room, office, or home.

The eight compass directions within a space govern various aspects of your life, so you place the corresponding colors, animals, numbers, and elements in the areas that you want to activate. The BSTB School, popularized in the past 20 years, uses the entrance to a room, house, or office as your main reference point. Using that point as your career area, you place objects in areas that correspond to the goals you want to achieve.

In both schools, the *bagua*, or octagon, is placed on the floor of a room or house and is stretched to accommodate the shape of the property. Both schools also instruct you to activate a particular aspect of your life by putting something in its corresponding area. For instance, adding two objects made of earth materials to the SW area enhances love and romance. However, that is where the similarities end, since each school handles a particular space differently.

The Compass School

In the Compass School, the eight areas of a room correspond to the same areas in adjoining rooms. Thus, N–NE–E–SE–S–SW–W–NW will always be the same in all rooms. The following list details the eight compass directions and what they represent in the Compass School:

North: Career, business success, black, winter, water, metal, tortoise, 1

Northeast: Knowledge, wisdom, self-development, success in school, turquoise, tan, winter becoming spring, earth, fire, 8

East: Family life, health, nutrition, harmony, prosperity, green, spring, wood, water, dragon, 3

Southeast: Wealth, prosperity, abundance, green, purple, spring becoming summer, wood, water, 4

South: Fame, fortune, longevity, festivity, joy, red, summer, fire, wood, bird, 9

Southwest: Marriage, mother, relationships, love, romance, spouse, yellow, white, pink, red, summer becoming autumn, earth, fire, 2

West: Children, children's fame, creativity, white, autumn, metal, earth, tiger, 7

Northwest: Supportive and helpful people, international trade and travel, interests outside the home, father, gray, metal, earth, autumn becoming winter, 6

INTRODUCTION

The BSTB School

In the BSTB School, the areas that correspond to aspects of your life change from room to room, depending upon the location of the most frequently used entrance to the room. Therefore, the wealth area changes from one spot to another in adjoining rooms, according to the locations of the entrances to those rooms. The list below explains the eight areas of a room (beginning at the wall shared by the main entrance and moving in a clockwise direction) and what they represent according to the BSTB School:

Front Center (at the entrance looking into the room): Career, business, work, water, fountains, black, white

Left Front: Knowledge, self-development, wisdom, success, goals, books, personal health, growth, blue, green, black

Left Center: Family, health, ancestors, relatives, family heirlooms, souvenirs, shrines to ancestors, photos, blue, green

Left Rear: Wealth, prosperity, abundance, material things, fountains, fish, things of value, aquariums, banners, red, purple, blue, green

Center Rear (across from the main entrance): Fame, fortune, awards, diplomas, fireplace, candles, red, green

Right Rear: Marriage, relationships, romance

Right Center: Children, creativity, round, metal, arts and crafts, toys, games, white, metal

Right Front: Supportive and helpful people, religious icons, travel, friends, black, white, gray

Using Feng Shui

I have created the acronym CANE — C for color; A for animal; N for number; E for element — to help you place objects according to general feng shui principles. Basically, place the C, A, N, and E in its corresponding direction if you want to improve that aspect of your life. You can also add the element that precedes it in the generative cycle to strengthen your efforts. To suppress an aspect, introduce its "destroyer," or the one that follows it in the destructive cycle, to weaken it.

Whichever form of feng shui you choose, be consistent and practical. If you don't get the results you desire, feel free to try other forms of the art. The guidelines are basically the same: Put the right objects in the right locations in order to achieve harmony with the universe, nature, and yourself. You can also activate the areas of your life that you wish to improve, such as health, career, or love.

Much of what you do is based on common sense, sound architectural design, intuition, geography, ecology, meteorology, astronomy, interior design, ancient Chinese philosophy, and Chinese folk beliefs. As you tap into the *tao*, or flow of the universe and its rhythms, these are the keys you will use to create a more holistic, natural, and simple way of life. Keep your heart pure and your intentions strong, and see how this fascinating and wonderful tradition transforms your life.

WHAT GOES
WHERE:
A TO Z

Do light your altar with artificial lights or candles to distinguish it as a special or holy location.

Do put your altar in a quiet location, away from the flow of traffic in the house. Your altar should have an undisturbed place of honor.

19

Do keep your altar indoors or covered under some sort of shelter.

Don't put your altar in an area that is near to, next to, under, or across from stairs or a bathroom.

Do place an altar across the room
from your front door or in the
NW area of a room or house.
The NW represents heaven and
father, the spiritual and temporal
heads of the household.

Don't put statues of deities in a low place. Choose a spot higher than the tallest person in the household.

Do clean and maintain your altar. Discard dried flowers, fruit, incense, and other offerings that are past their prime.

Do be mindful of the original purpose or use of an old or second-hand item. For example, avoid masks of the dead that were used for burials or exorcisms, or statues that have come from tombs, caves, pyramids, cemeteries, or temples.

Do purify antiques with wind, water, fire, sound, salt, or other techniques outside of your home before bringing them inside.

Don't bring purchases from flea markets or tag sales into your home if the previous owners are deceased, divorced, or bankrupt; have been fired from jobs; or have experienced other misfortunes.

Do put an aquarium in N areas (associated with business success and career growth) or in E or SE areas for prosperity. In every corner of the world, water — in the form of rivers, lakes, and oceans — has brought trade, commerce, and prosperity.

Do use a metal and glass (or acrylic) aquarium in N areas. In the generative cycle of the elements, metal creates water.

Don't put an aquarium in or facing a bathroom or a bedroom. This is considered unlucky and can result in loss of fortune.

Don't keep an aquarium in your kitchen. Since the kitchen is in the domain of fire and is nourished by wood, the element of water will destroy your prosperity.

Do keep fish in multiples of nine, a symbol of long life, or in odd numbers. Eight fish should be gold in color, since eight is the homonym for the Chinese verb "to prosper." One fish should be black, a color that will provide protection and absorb negative energy.

Don't fret if any of your fish die, for it means that the deceased animal has absorbed something negative that would have happened to you. Replace the fish as soon as you can to maintain your protection.

Do keep one arrowana, known as the "prosperity fish." Arrowanas are beautiful silver, gold, or black-tinged ribbonlike fish from Southeast Asia. They are very auspicious, but they are tropical and need water heated to about 82°F in order to survive. Place your arrowana in N, W, SE, and NW areas to activate wealth.

Do keep an odd number of fish; this represents yang energy.

Do keep your
aquarium at a
level about
waist-high.

Do keep your aquarium and its water clean and keep the pumps, filters, and other equipment in good working order.

Don't hang pictures
of family members,
especially those who are
deceased, on the wall
above your aquarium.

Don't locate a bedroom in the basement. Finish basement rooms for occasional use only — as a family room, guest room, or game room.

Do keep your
basement
free of clutter.

Don't choose a home in which the bathroom, and particularly the toilet, is located in the SE, E, or S (the areas of wealth and prosperity) or the SW (the area of marriage and relationships).

Do hang mirrors on the outside of the bathroom door if the bathroom happens to be in a wealth area. Put a wind chime in the window to dam the flow of water, or energy, from the house.

Don't buy or rent a house in which the bathroom is located above the front entrance. This portends major calamity to the family.

Don't have a bathroom that extends beyond the main door to your home. If you do, your wealth will drain out of the house. This predicament can be mitigated by painting the bathroom an earth color, such as yellow, tan, orange, or brown; using accessories made from porcelain, clay, china, or terra cotta; and using earth-colored towels.

(43)

Do make sure your toilet, if it is enclosed in its own space, has a door to close it off. Remember that the original name for the toilet was *water closet!*

Do keep the seats, covers, and doors to bathrooms shut at all times, especially if the toilet faces a bedroom or directly faces the bathroom door, because toilets emanate negative energy.

Don't put a bathroom across from your kitchen, which represents the prosperity of the family, or across from the main entrance, where positive energy enters the home. Don't put a bathroom at the center of the house, which represents the heart of a home.

Do hang a wind chime that is made of an earth material, such as terra cotta or porcelain, or that has five solid clay rods if your bathroom is in the N. This will keep your business and career success from going "down the drain."

Don't spend tremendous amounts of time or money on this area of the home. Keep the décor commensurate with the function: simple! Your resources are better concentrated on more important areas of your home, such as the master bedroom, kitchen, study, and office.

Do create a safe haven for sleep, rest, intimacy, and recharging your spirit and body.

Don't keep more than a few books in your bedroom; they are too stimulating.

Don't use lots of yang colors, such as gold or red, in a bedroom. These colors stimulate your energy, resulting in poor sleep.

Do take notice of the view that
greets you when you awaken.
What's outside your bedroom
window — a lamppost, church
spire, neighboring rooftops, or a
corner of your neighbor's house?
Are any of them "poison" arrows
disturbing your sleep or rest? If
so, use a concave *bagua* mirror to
absorb their negative energy.

Do remove as much electronic equipment from your bedroom as possible, especially televisions, VCRs, stereos, and computers, which emit electromagnetic energy that is detrimental to rest, health, and fertility.

Don't use an electric blanket or sleep on a water bed. The former generates electromagnetic energy, and the latter is believed to cause arthritis, muscle pain, and joint problems.

Don't use round windows, skylights, or unusual ceilings in a bedroom, as these shapes create odd pockets that collect negative energy.

Do avoid sleeping in a bedroom situated above a garage, which channels the noxious fumes from the automobiles to the room's occupants, affecting health.

Don't occupy a bedroom that is in a direct line with a straight road. If a vehicle's headlights shine at or into the bedroom at night, use the room for exercise, storage, sewing, computer work, play, or other leisure activities instead.

Do use plants and flowers to introduce healing yang energy into an ill or convalescing person's bedroom.

Don't keep a broom in the bedroom of a dying person; brooms are believed to sweep away life.

Do keep your bedroom free of clutter and minimize the amount of furniture so that *chi*, or life energy, can flow easily throughout the room.

Don't have any water features, such as fountains or aquariums, in your bedroom, where they are considered unlucky and can lead to loss of wealth.

Do cleanse the energy in your bedroom several times a year with wind (airing), sound (music, bells), fire (smudging with incense), or water (misting all walls with purified or holy water). Use the form of energy cleansing that matches the upcoming season — water for spring and winter, fire for summer, and metal-generated sound for autumn.

Do clean your bedroom (or house) during a new moon, at the solstices (March 21, June 21, September 21, and December 21), or whenever the atmosphere feels heavy, stale, or hostile, such as after an argument, illness, or death on the premises.

Do air out a bedroom (or house) thoroughly for at least an hour after smudging. Open all the doors and windows, so that the negative energy is drawn outside and dispersed.

Do close any bathroom doors and toilet seat covers if a bathroom leads into your bedroom. This simple habit can ensure a good night's sleep.

Don't install a ceiling fan directly above a bed, where it will adversely influence the health of the occupants underneath. A ceiling fan can be situated past the foot of the bed, where it can still effectively cool a room without affecting the people sleeping in it.

Do encourage your child to study in the NE area of his or her bedroom to facilitate learning and achieve scholarly success.

Do remove pornographic, violent, warlike, depressing, or lewd posters and publications from a young person's bedroom if you want him or her to achieve success in school and life.

Don't keep too many plants or any plants that have sharp foliage, such as cactus, in your bedroom. Plants emit yang energy that can disturb high-quality rest.

Do position your bed so that it is not in line with the entrance to your bedroom, especially if your feet point toward that entrance. This is almost universally considered a "death position," because those who die at home are carried out of a room or house feet first.

Don't place the head of your bed against a wall shared with a bathroom.

Don't put the head of your bed against a window unless there is a solid headboard, curtain, drapes, blinds, or shutters to block off the window. Energy enters the body through the head; this holy part of the body needs protection and support in the form of something visually solid.

Do use a headboard made of wood, metal, or foam. Match its shape to the element associated with the direction of the room — arches and round shapes for W and NW; rectangles and squares for E and SE; curvy, wavy, or irregular shapes for N; and triangular shapes for S.

Don't position a bed on the short wall of a room with a pitched ceiling. The energy of the sloping ceiling will press down on the bed's occupant.

DON'T

Do make sure that the corners of desks, shelves, cabinets, wardrobes, other furniture, and architectural features do not point toward the bed. These corners resemble the points of arrows and represent *sha*, or "killing" energy.

Do choose bedding and linens in solid colors. If they have patterns, avoid geometric, angular designs that emanate negative energy and disturb your rest.

Don't use twin beds pushed together or twin box springs under your king-sized mattress if you share your bed with someone. These arrangements symbolize a split in your relationship. If you have twin box springs, tie the adjoining legs together securely with red cord so that they will not separate.

DON'T

Don't place your bed under a beam. If this cannot be helped, install a false ceiling with fabric, or hang wind chimes, flutes, or red fringe on the beam. Beams symbolize separation if they appear between a bed's occupants, and they represent health problems in the area of the body that they bisect.

Don't move the bed of a pregnant woman, as this may disturb the life energy present in the bed that led to the conception.

Do ring a bell in the corners of a room to clear stagnant or stale energy.

Do use bells with pleasant tinkling sounds to activate yang energy in your home.

Do give your bell a single, firm shake above a person's head. Then, holding it about six inches away, trace the person's body from head to toe to cleanse his or her energy.

Do choose bells that are new and have a wooden handle for cleansing activities. Select brass and silver bells in the sounds or tones that appeal to you.

Do clean your bells by wiping them after each use. Store them in W areas, as W represents the element of metal.

Don't use bells in the E or SE, which are both wood areas and are destroyed by metal.

Do use bells in
the metal areas
of W and NW
or across from
an entrance.

BELLS

Do string one or three bells with auspicious red ribbon, thread, or cord. Hang the ribbon on your doorknob or above your door, so that the bells sound joyously whenever someone enters. Bells attract good luck and good fortune.

Don't select bells that have been used inside temples or churches. They have absorbed the energy of those with sin, and you'll bring that negative energy into your home.

DON'T

Do keep a red bird, such as a parrot, in S areas. Red is the traditional Chinese color for protection.

Don't ask for feathers from others.

Do hang feathers that you find near your front door. These feathers represent protection for you and your family. If your feathers blow away, try to find others to replace them.

Don't keep your pet bird caged.
Confining it means that your
wealth will be limited.

Don't throw feathers
away if you find them.

Do keep birds in the SW when they are in pairs to strengthen your romance, love, marriage, or motherhood area.

Do put a pair of metal cranes in the N area of your garden with a water element. The crane has long been associated with good fortune, wealth, wisdom, and longevity for the patriarch and matriarch of a family.

Do use a statue of a rooster to offset the divisive effects of ceiling beams and interior pillars and posts. The bird's beak should be aimed directly at the offending spot.

Do use a ceramic rooster to mitigate the dreaded symbol of illness and affliction, the centipede. A "centipede" is a lamppost outside your house or window that has three or more crosspieces intersecting the main posts. Point the rooster's beak directly toward the centipede.

Do put doves carved in wood in S areas to fuel the element of fire there and increase longevity.

Do improve your relationship with your partner by putting a pair of Mandarin ducks, a male and a female, in SW areas. These ducks represent marital devotion, fidelity, and happiness because they are deeply attached to each other. When separated, the birds are believed to pine away to the point of death.

Do use two wild geese, which always fly in pairs, in the relationship and marriage area of your bedroom, the SW. These animals are messengers of good news and represent the married state.

Do use figurines of a pair of lovebirds in the SW corner of your home, garden, or bed-room to enhance the romance aspect of your life.

Do put statues of eagles or hawks outside and away from your house for protection. Good locations are at the bottom of a driveway or on either side of a gate.

Don't display statues, pictures, or other images of predatory birds with their victims clasped in their talons, or hovering about their dead or half-eaten prey.

Do use magpies as decorations in S areas. They are harbingers of joy, happiness, and festivity and are good luck omens, for they always bring happy news. If they set up residence near your home, in your trees, or under your eaves, good fortune is sure to follow.

Do place the phoenix in SW areas to attract happy relationships and marriage. This bird personifies everything good and beautiful and is believed to appear only when China is governed by a just, reasonable, and fair ruler, or during peaceful and prosperous times.

Do put a phoenix or a pheasant, another symbol of beauty, in the S area to attract fame and fortune. One carved in wood is doubly powerful because the wood element nourishes the fire element of S.

Do place a swallow in E (wood) or S (fire) areas to enhance your prosperity and good fortune. The swallow, which builds its nest under the eaves of buildings, portends approaching success or a lucky change in the fortunes and affairs of the house's occupants.

Do pick a laughing Buddha for your home or business. He is the cheerful, chubby chap with a pot-belly, carrying a gourd or a bag hanging from a staff held over one shoulder, and sometimes an ingot in one hand. The bag contains your troubles and problems, which he has collected for you.

Do select the largest-sized Buddha that appeals to you, keeping him in proportion to the size of the room in which he's located.

Do display a Buddha with children climbing all over him. This represents an abundance of good fortune coming from heaven.

Don't put your Buddha
on the ground so that
people look down on
him. Keep him level
with or higher than the
occupants of a room.

Do position your Buddha diagonally across from and facing the door, which is the position of power and honor in the room.

Don't bring a used or antique
statue or figurine of the Buddha,
especially one from a temple, into
your home unless you cleanse or
purify it first. It may carry
unwanted negative energy.

DON'T

Do use scented candles to purify a room, help you relax, and improve your sleep.

Don't use candles
in the metal
element areas
of W and NW:
Fire melts metal.

Do light red, blue, or purple candles in S areas to stimulate celebrity, fame, fortune, reputation, happiness, and festivity; light white, yellow, orange, pink, or red candles to reinforce the SW area, which represents love, marriage, relationships, motherhood, and romance.

Do put blue, green, or turquoise candles in the NE area to enhance knowledge, scholarly success, wisdom, experience, and self-development.

Do choose an automobile in a color that matches your element. If you are a wood person, choose blue or green. A fire person should choose a shade of red. Metal-element people should select white, gray, silver, or gold metallic finishes, and earth folks should pick out beige or tan. Water-element car owners should select blue, teal, or black.

Do use air fresheners with a favorite scent inside your car. Pleasant aromas create a sense of peace and serenity — a valuable commodity when you are stuck in traffic or stressed out or just need a lift!

Do play inspirational, educational, or uplifting tapes to stimulate your mind and spirit while you are in your vehicle. You can productively use your hours behind the wheel to foster your personal or professional growth.

Do tie three coins, either ancient Chinese coins or silver dollars, together with red cord or string and hang them on the inside of the main door to your home. This gesture keeps your prosperity inside your home and is especially effective if your front entrance faces one of the metal directions, W or NW.

Don't hang any coins on your back door; this represents your money leaving the premises!

DON'T

Do wear nine Chinese coins in any combination of jewelry, such as earrings, bracelets, brooches, or rings, to attract good fortune.

Do tape three Chinese coins to the underside of your telephone to encourage it to ring more often. Or hang a hollow-rod wind chime or crystal above the telephone.

Do use aqua or turquoise in the NE to enhance knowledge, wisdom, self-development, and experience, and in the E to promote family, harmony, health, nutrition, growth, vitality, prosperity, and youth.

Do use brown, beige, or tan to represent spring, youth, prosperity, family, harmony, nutrition, strength, growth, and vitality.

Don't use black in bedrooms or on the walls or ceilings of any room, and don't combine it with yellow or use it in an earth area (SW or NE). In the N, it enhances business success, career, and new beginnings, but it also represents mourning, evil, and guilt.

Do use blue, especially ultramarine, in the N to attract business success, and in the E to enhance family, harmony, growth, and health.

Don't use blue in the earth areas (SW and NE) or wear it in a ribbon or bow in your hair; it is one of the traditional Chinese mourning symbols.

Do use metallic gold in the W to enhance children, children's fame, creativity, business and career success, supportive people, trade, travel, prosperity, wealth, and interests outside the home.

Don't use metallic gold in bedrooms, as it destroys health and harmony, or in E areas (representing health, prosperity, and family) or SE areas (representing wealth and prosperity).

Do use nonmetallic gold in NE areas to enhance wisdom, knowledge, and scholarly success. It also enhances SW (the area of marriage, motherhood, love, and relationships).

Don't use nonmetallic gold in the N, which represents business and career success. Nonmetallic gold represents earth and earth destroys water, the symbol of financial prosperity.

Do use green, the color of health, harmony, prosperity, youth, growth, spring, wealth, and prosperity, to enhance S areas (representing fame, fortune, joy, festivity, and protection from evil).

DON'T

Don't use green in earth areas (SW and NE). Green symbolizes wood, which destroys earth.

Don't use gray in wood areas (E and SE). Gray represents metal, which destroys wood.

DON'T

Do use gray in NW, N, and W areas to enhance supportive people, benefactors, mentors, international trade, trips, travel, and interests outside the home.

Do use orange in
SW areas to promote
motherhood, romance,
love, relationships, and
marriage.

Don't use orange in
N areas. Orange is a fire
color; if placed in the
N, it will be doused
by water, that area's
element.

Do use peach liberally in your unmarried daughter's bedroom so that she will marry well; it is the color used by single women to attract a good husband. If you can find peonies or pictures with this color, put them outside her bedroom.

Don't use peach in your bedroom if you are already married. This hue will activate your partner's roving eye or heart, causing infidelity.

Do use pink in a single woman's bedroom; it represents romance, love, and marriage. It is especially powerful in S and SW areas.

Do use purple, the color of knowledge, wisdom, intelligence, wealth, and spirituality, in the E to enhance harmony, prosperity, family, and health, or in the SE to promote wealth and prosperity.

Do use red in any form in S areas. Next to black, it is the most powerful yang color in Chinese culture. It represents fame, fortune, joy, festivity, longevity, summer, passion, and protection from bad luck and evil.

Do use red for newly-weds, brides, people celebrating their birth-days, temple doors, baby blankets, fire-crackers, embroideries, and tapestries.

Do use red hearts and silk flowers in the SW, the area of relationships, marriage, love, romance, and motherhood, or the S, the area of fame, fortune, long life, reputation, and prosperity. Tie two red cords or ribbons on the inside of your bedroom doorknob if you'd like to attract a serious partner.

Don't use too much red in a bedroom. Its yang energy is too active and will disturb the occupant's rest.

Do put a wooden figure of a wish-fulfilling cow on your desk in the SE or E area. Or use a metal figure in the W or SW, or a ceramic one in SW or NE locations. These placements will encourage wealth. The cow represents spring and is revered because it pulls the plow to prepare the fields from which the harvest comes.

Do clear your new crystals by running them under cold water (preferably sea, holy, or purified water; don't use tap water) to wash away the energies of all the people who have handled them before you. Let the water drip down from the point.

Do purify natural crystals before using them by gently rinsing them in rainwater, the ocean, or a solution of sea salt and cold water (mixed in a glass or ceramic container, not a metal or plastic one). Or bury them in the earth for at least three days and up to one moon cycle or store them under pyramids.

Don't keep your colored crystals in the sunlight, as it will cause them to fade.

Do recharge your crystals by placing them out in the moonlight as often as you can.

Do hang two white, red, gold, or pink heart-shaped crystals in the SW corner of your bedroom to activate love, marriage, and relationships.

DO

Do put crystals in multiples of eight in the NE area of your office or study if you want to excel in your work or increase your intuitive and thinking powers. Put them in the NE area of your child's bedroom to help her or him do well academically.

Do use crystals in the earth areas of SW (marriage, relationships, romance, love), the earth area of NE (knowledge, wisdom, self-development), and especially the metal area of W, because earth creates metal, which is made into coins and represents wealth.

Do place six crystal balls in the NW, another metal area, to bring supportive people into your life and to strengthen the power and influence of the male head of the household.

Do hang a crystal from an exposed beam, or from a door-frame if you have three doors in a row in a hallway. Crystals break up the negative energy created by beams and long hallways.

Do hang a crystal in a dark corner to activate *chi*, or life energy, in that location.

Do put a crystal jar or
vase on a desk to deflect
sha, or "killing" energy,
if the desk is in line
with a door or corridor.

Do dangle a crystal from a window if the view includes corners of buildings, rooftops, lampposts, chimneys, or other unpleasant sights.

Do clean your birth gemstone after each use to keep its energy pure.

Do collect citrine crystals to tuck inside your wallet or purse, as this stone is associated with wealth and fortune.

Do display a figure of a deer in the proper direction. Place it in W or NW areas if it is metal, in E or SE locations if it is carved from wood, and in the NE or SW if it is crafted from an earth material, such as clay, porcelain, or terra cotta. The deer represents long life, speed, prosperity, endurance, and wealth.

Do examine the view that you have while sitting at your desk. You should not directly face a "killing" arrow, such as a head-on road, the curve of a highway, a lamppost, a fire hydrant, the space between two buildings, a steeple, a rooftop, a tree trunk, power lines and transformers, the edges of signs and billboards, or the corner of a building.

Do use a desk that has the auspicious dimensions of 35" × 60" × 33" (89 × 152 × 84 cm).

Do use a wooden or glass desk in the E and a metal or stone desk in the W.

DO

Do try to have more space in front of your desk than behind it. You need the support of a wall behind you and space in front of you to allow good *chi* to beat a clear path to you and your business.

DO

DO

Don't position your desk directly in line with the door or under a beam. If you do, you will be receiving negative *sha* energy or will be located under oppressive *sha*, which causes illness, accidents, and misfortune.

Do buy a new desk or use one whose previous owner prospered.

Don't put bizarre or strange objects on your desk, as these attract negative energy.

167

Do place any of the following on your desk to attract good luck and prosperity: a wish-fulfilling cow, deer, dragon, tortoise, unicorn, money tree, prosperity plant, table-top fountain, crystal paperweight, or candy jar.

Do keep a bowl or an arrangement of fruit on your dining room table to represent continuous sustenance to your family. Add a mirror on the W or NW wall of your dining room to double the food on your table.

Do put images of food and fruit in the E area of your dining room to represent the abundance and sustenance that you want to attract to your table and your home.

Don't hang too many pictures of birds and other feathered creatures in your dining room, as this will create an imbalance in yang energy.

Do ensure family harmony with the proper seating arrangements. The father sits in the NW, the mother in the SW, the eldest son in the E, the eldest daughter in the SE, the youngest son in the NE, the youngest daughter in the W, the middle son in the N, and the middle daughter in the S. Chinese dinner tables are round to accommodate these arrangements.

Do place persimmons in S areas to symbolize joy and festivity.

Don't leave cleaning supplies in the dining room. They symbolize the "cleaning out" of one's income, good health, nutrition, and prosperity.

Do put a figure of a dog in the direction that matches the element from which the figure is made. Put a metal dog in a W or NW area, a wooden dog in the E or SE, and a dog made of an earth material in the NE or SW. The dog symbolizes faithfulness and is valued as both a protector and a scavenger.

Do place statues of dogs at your door for protection and to guard your prosperity.

Do adopt a stray dog if one comes to your home. "A dog that comes on its own" is a very lucky omen that sustenance, fortune, or wealth will arrive on your doorstep.

Do make sure you have a clear view from the front entrance of your home, in order to facilitate a clear view of the world.

Do use a small round or octagonal mirror or a shiny, flat metal doorknocker to deflect "poison" arrows, such as tree trunks, lampposts, fire hydrants, corners of neighboring buildings, church steeples, or other objects projecting *sha* energy toward your home or obstructing your view.

Don't use an all-glass front door; choose a solid door instead. A small, beveled window on the door is acceptable. Too much glass does not offer protection for the home and allows prosperity to leak out.

Do place a dragon in the E area of a living room, family room, library, office, or study or on the E corner of a desk. The dragon is the traditional Chinese symbol of growth, protection, vitality, spring, prosperity, health, and new beginnings.

Don't put a dragon, an animal with a lot of yang energy, in your bedroom, which should always be restful, peaceful, and serene.

Don't face your dragon toward the N, as this is considered unlucky.

Do use dragons as decorations if you were born in the Year of the Dragon.

183

Do choose dragons or pictures of dragons that resemble the qualities of water: slick, shiny, translucent, and the color of the sea. This is more helpful than a dragon made of wood, china, or porcelain, though all materials are acceptable.

Do have your dragon facing a source of clean water, such as a lake, river, ocean, beach, waterfall, or fountain.

Do use arrangements of just one dragon, which represents power; a group of two dragons, symbolizing unity; or a group of nine dragons, which promotes longevity.

Do choose a turquoise dragon. Red is the second-best color for a dragon, and gold is third.

Do place your dragon at eye level, so you can see it easily. It will then provide you with strength and vitality.

Don't put your dragon in, facing, or near the bathroom or laundry room. These rooms represent dirty water.

Do combine your dragon with a phoenix. This represents a happy, harmonious pairing of partners and is a popular traditional wedding symbol in China.

Don't buy or use a carpet that has dragon designs on it. Dragons must be able to fly free and are unable to do so if they are being stepped on.

Do use a kneeling ceramic elephant on your altar. The elephant symbolizes longevity, power, strength, wisdom, and high moral standards and is one of Buddhism's seven sacred treasures.

Do put an elephant in S (the direction associated with long life), E, and SE areas if it is crafted of wood. Put it in NE and SW areas if it is made of porcelain, terra cotta, or china.

Do place pairs of standing or kneeling elephants as guardians flanking the doors of your home on either the outside or the inside.

Do balance quiet activities, such as board games, card games, reading, and puzzles, with active pursuits, including table tennis, television, billiards, and video games, in a family room.

Do use muted but warm colors, such as yellow or green, the color of harmony, in a family room to foster creativity, teamwork, and relationships.

195

Do use round tables to represent family harmony and equality.

Do put fertility symbols and images to work in several areas:

> SW (motherhood)
> NW (fatherhood)
> W (children)
> E (family life)

Do use a pair of chopsticks, which literally mean "quick children" in Chinese, to enhance fertility. Use red wooden chopsticks in the SW; metal chopsticks in NW and W areas; and wooden, bamboo, or lacquer chopsticks in E locations.

Do point the chopstick tips away from you and never display them stuck vertically in a bowl of anything, such as rice. Standing up like this, the two chopsticks portend bad luck, as they resemble sticks of incense placed at the feet of a deceased person at a wake.

FERTILITY

Do use images of elephants to enhance fertility. Use bronze, gold, copper, pewter, silver, or other metal elephants in the W and NW; use wooden elephants in E, SE, and S areas; use clay, terra cotta, china, porcelain, or stone elephants in SW and NE locations; and use crystal elephants in the N. Touch and rub the elephant regularly.

Do place a stuffed white or yellow tiger, or a small picture of a resting or benign tiger with or without cubs, in the W area of your home or bedroom to increase the size of your family. Tigers represent children. The tiger images you use need not be large or obtrusive, but the tigers should be in a dignified pose.

Don't decorate your home with images of fierce, stalking, pouncing, or attacking tigers, with or without live or dead prey, if you wish to have children.

Do use traditional Chinese fertility symbols, such as a picture of 100 children, a laughing Buddha statue with children climbing all over him, a pomegranate, lotus seeds, or a statue of Kwan Yin, the Goddess of Mercy, who represents hearth, fertility, children, and home.

Do fill a covered earthen jar with raw rice and put it in SW areas to expand your family.

Don't cut any trees or remove any hills or mounds in the NW area of your property, as they represent the support and protection of the father.

Do paint the SW wall of your bedroom a shade of yellow, which symbolizes motherhood. Or paint the W and NW walls white for fatherhood.

Do put yellow, pink, or red orchids in a clay or terra cotta pot in a SW area if you desire children. Or, put white or yellow orchids in a metal container in W areas. Orchids symbolize the perfect man, love, beauty, refinement, and many offspring.

DO

Do decorate your daughter's bed-room with fresh peonies or with photographs, illustrations, or paintings of peonies. This will attract good men to her life.

Don't keep pictures of peonies in your home after all the single women have married.

Do use jasmine, which represents women and sweetness, in W areas.

209

Don't have pictures or vases of peonies in your bedroom if you are already married. This flower will encourage your partner to stray or seek love interests outside your home.

Do use narcissus, plum blossoms, hyacinths, and orchids for enhancing relationships. Place them in the SW and give them as gifts during the Chinese New Year.

Do match the color of your chrysanthemums to the area in which you place them. For example, place purple flowers in the SE for wealth and prosperity. Chrysanthemums symbolize longevity, dependability, and the desire for a long duration of anything wonderful, such as a marriage or career.

Do pair chrysanthemums with plum blossoms to symbolize an easy life from birth to retirement. Group them with nine quails to symbolize harmony and peace for the next nine generations of a family.

Do combine a single lotus blossom with a bud to represent the ideal partnership. The lotus flower is the ultimate symbol of Buddhism and represents purity, joy, and perfection. Because its exquisite blossoms grow from the mud at the bottom of ditches, lakes, and ponds, it exemplifies the possibility that perfection can come from impurity.

Do combine a lotus blossom with a magpie to relay wishes for scholarly success to someone.

Do place a lotus blossom with a *koi*, a member of the carp family, in the arms of a young boy to express your wishes for good fortune. This fish is valued for the unique markings on its back and its Chinese name, *li*, is a homonym for the word "prosperity."

Do use narcissus in E or SE areas. A traditional symbol of good fortune for the year to follow, narcissus bulbs are forced to bloom at the Chinese New Year. They are used for decoration and as a gift to wish someone good luck in a business or a career.

Don't decorate your home, especially your bedroom, with dried flowers, branches, grasses, or potpourri. These dead objects generate yin energy that can adversely affect your love life!

Do give freshly cut flowers to those who are ill. This brings them much-needed healing yang energy. Replace the old flowers with fresh ones when the blooms wilt or fade.

Don't keep an overabundance of flowers or plants in your bedroom, as they create lots of yang energy in what needs to be a yin environment to foster good rest. Three small plants in the E are quite sufficient to produce oxygen and promote health, well-being, harmony, and family accord.

Do plant red flowers in the ground or in planters on both sides of a front entrance that faces S. This provides protection to your family.

DO

Do plant flowers on both sides of a straight footpath if it runs directly from your front door to the street. This strategy will soften the straight line of negative *sha* energy by slowing it down.

Do plant or place two tall flowering shrubs on either side of a tree that emanates *sha* energy directly in line with your front door. This creates a triangle pointed away from your home and neutralizes the effect of the "killing" arrow.

Don't use the image of a fox in your home; it is too fierce and brings a lot of negative energy. The cunning fox often symbolizes a demon.

Do use a fox
outdoors for
protection.

Don't forget the most basic law of gardening and life: You reap what you sow. Plant and nurture seeds of kindness, honesty, compassion, and integrity, and that's what you will harvest.

Do remember that your garden is a microcosm of the world.

Do plan a new view, surprise, or delight to be revealed at every step or turn along a garden path.

Do incorporate curving paths, which bring beneficial energy and draw visitors further into your garden.

Do achieve a balance of yin and yang, light and dark, and soft and hard through the various materials and plants used in your garden. Your garden should have private and public areas, as well as active and meditative ones.

Do endeavor to create a garden that looks and feels as natural as possible.

Do use colors that are subtle, soothing, and harmonious.

Do treasure the natural flora and fauna, disturb them as little as possible, and use them to their fullest potential.

Do share the blessings and abundance of your garden, whether it is in the form of fruits, flowers, herbs, or vegetables.

Do create mounds or hills if your property is flat, so that it will not have too much yin energy. Add trees, bushes, walls, or hedges to provide balancing yang energy.

Do use metal, glass, gold, mirrors, fountains, waterfalls, and ponds in the N area of your garden, which is associated with water and is enhanced by metal. This area also represents business, career, creativity, personal growth, new ideas, inspiration, music, art, and intuition.

Don't use stones, boulders, clay, brick, ceramics, tile, marble, geodes, or anything else from the earth in the N area of your garden.

Do use stones, clay, brick or ceramics in the NE area of your garden. This area, which is associated with earth and enhanced by fire, is a good place for stone benches or walls, terra cotta decorations, sundials, or a rock garden. It also represents knowledge, meditation, spiritual and intellectual growth, nature, research, and experimentation.

Don't use anything wooden in the NE or SW areas of your garden.

Do plant prize specimens of anything you grow for income in the SE, the area governing wealth.

Do use fountains, waterfalls, ponds, wooden furniture or steps, decks, trellises, and arbors in the E and SE areas of your garden, which are associated with wood and enhanced by water. The E represents family, health, peace, growth, rebirth, harmony; the SE represents prosperity, abundance, communication, and perseverance.

Do burn your leaves
in the S area of your
garden.

Don't use metal, glass, gold, or
mirrors in the E or SE area of
your garden.

Do use lights, statues of animals, pointed shapes that represent the tips of flames, wooden furniture, pointed trees, pagodas, or a barbecue in the S area of your garden, which is associated with fire and enhanced by wood. The S represents fame, fortune, festivity, opportunity, dreams, awards, longevity, festivity, and reputation.

Don't use the S area of your garden for water elements, including fountains, waterfalls, and ponds.

DON'T

Do place lights, low buildings, stones, ceramics, marble, or earth materials in multiples of two in the SW area of your garden, which is associated with metal and enhanced by fire. This area represents marriage, relationships, motherhood, and love. The SW is a great place for two hammocks, romantic symbols, or a team sports area.

Do put a compost pile, children's garden, or playground with metal equipment in the W area of your garden. This area represents children, children's fame, creativity, harvest, and socializing. It's a good site for sunbathing, convalescing, and entertaining.

Do put stone or metal statues of deities, a tool shed, or metal outdoor furniture in the NW area. NW represents travel, helpful people, trade, interests outside the home, fatherhood, mentors, benefactors, supporters, and friends.

Don't allow any form of fire, including a barbecue grill or candles, in the W or NW area of your garden.

Do use an iron gate with an open design in the S area to allow beneficial energy to move freely. Triangles and pyramid designs are great, but do not select designs that have spikes or points at the top of the gate, as they will create *sha* energy.

247

Do use a gate in the SW only if it is about as high as your waist or chest. Choose one with a design of squares to match the earth element.

Do use full-height metal gates in the W to slow down and obstruct the extreme yang energy of the afternoon sun. Use circular, semi-circular, and arch designs in this direction.

Do use arches, semicircles, and circles in blue or black metal for your NW gate.

Do use a square gate in the NE, since this shape represents the earth.

Do take your inspiration from water and the sea as you select your N gate; one embellished with waves and curves is ideal.

Do use rectangles, cylinders, columns, and poles in the design of your gate in the E, where the element that reigns is wood.

Don't use any metal in your SE gate; use wood instead.

Do give a Chinese unicorn, or
chi ling, as a present to bestow
good wishes upon someone.
This unicorn, which bears almost
no resemblance to its European
counterpart, is the symbol of
goodness, long life, peace, harmony,
protection, many children, and an
unending family line.

Do give bird feathers as a thoughtful gift to your family and friends, as they represent protection.

Do give a lion as a gift for a new home to provide protection to the family.

Don't give a bell, a clock, or anything with a clock's face as a gift. These are akin to gifts of scissors, knives, or swords and symbolize the severing of a relationship or a life.

Do attach a penny to each blade if you give a gift of a pair of scissors or a set of knives or swords. This neutralizes the severance effect. The pennies must be returned to the giver.

Do give a gift of a jade dove or pigeon, a symbol of long life, to bestow best wishes for health and longevity.

DO

Do give potted kumquat, tanger-
ine, or orange plants laden with
fruit to new business owners, or to
friends and family during the
Chinese New Year. These gifts
symbolize prosperity, wealth, and
abundance in the months to come.

261

Do give lucky red money envelopes generously and freely as gifts; they are traditional and appropriate for happy events, including birthdays, anniversaries, weddings, housewarmings, engagements, the Chinese New Year, graduations, new businesses, births, and visiting family members after an absence. It is customary to put paper currency or a check inside.

Do make a homemade jade plant
by threading and twisting gold wire
into semiprecious stone "leaves"
on an artificial, potted bonsai tree.
Give the plant as a gift to express
wishes for prosperity and abundance. These stone trees are perfect
for placement in the earth areas of
NE and SW.

Do make a homemade money tree by hanging fan-folded, new currency with red thread on a silk tree. This makes a perfect gift for special occasions, such as a wedding, birthday, graduation, or new enterprise. Sometimes these artificial trees are festooned with miniature gold ingots or lucky red money envelopes.

Don't give a regular
bonsai plant as a gift,
since it symbolizes
limited growth and is
therefore unlucky.

Do give a sack of rice as a housewarming gift, as the Filipinos do, to bestow blessings of abundance. Rice represents survival, prosperity, sustenance, and fertility.

Do donate books
that you no longer use,
want, or need to schools,
churches, hospitals,
halfway homes, libraries,
prisons, or other
institutions.

Don't position a bed in line with the door in a bedroom at the end of a long hallway. Such a hallway is a conduit of negative, "killing" energy.

Do make sure that doors opening onto a hallway don't bang against one another. These "arguing doors" can cause quarrels and fighting within a household.

Don't darken your hallway with an excess of art and family pictures. Keep a balance of empty spaces and hanging objects.

Do add mirrors and light-colored artwork to hallways.

Do hang a picture opposite a door that opens onto a view of a wall.

Do use a group of eight horses, which represents the fabled eight horses that a Chinese emperor used to win a war.

Don't use groupings of five horses, as five is a very powerful yin number.

Do place your horse so that it faces S, the most yang direction.

Don't place a horse from a Chinese tomb, or a replica of a horse from a Chinese tomb, in your home, especially in the wealth, health, or marriage areas. These are funereal pieces that connote death and are therefore considered unlucky.

Do choose a stately horse that is standing or posing calmly with its head level or lifted. Or select a galloping horse that symbolizes vigor and strength.

Don't use a horse that is bucking or rearing up as if in fear, especially in your bedroom.

Do arrange your kitchen with a wall behind the stove, rather than placing the stove on an island or peninsula. The wall provides solid, continual support to the prosperity of your family. If you are not planning to remodel soon, use decorative stove covers or screens, available at kitchenware shops, to create a wall effect.

Do keep the burners of your stove clean and in good working order at all times. They represent the prosperity of your family and are of the utmost importance. The more burners in your kitchen, the more wealth you will enjoy.

Don't install more than one stove. Rather than doubling your wealth, this will divide it. Instead, increase the number of burners on the stovetop.

Do face either E (wood) or S (fire) when you are standing at your stove. In ancient civilizations, people burned wood to create the fire with which to cook their food.

Don't have the stove and the sink directly across from each other if one is on an island or peninsula, as water will destroy fire and this represents destruction of your family's wealth.

Don't have the stove and the sink too close together on the same counter, as water destroys fire.

Do hang a metal wind chime with five hollow rods over your stove to double your money.

Don't arrange your home so that you can see the kitchen as you enter the front door of your house. If you do, you will be preoccupied with food and may find yourself battling weight problems.

Don't leave too many things on kitchen surfaces in plain sight, as this will detract from a good flow of energy.

Do keep brooms, mops, garbage cans, and other cleaning tools, supplies, and equipment out of sight when not in use.

Do put your most often used utensils in the areas that correspond to their elements. For example, water in N, wood in E and SE, and metal in W and NW.

Don't place your refrigerator in the wood areas of E or SE. Although this major appliance stores and preserves food, which provides nutrition and is normally associated with E, it is manufactured out of metal, which destroys the wood element.

Do cover your family's rice storage container to protect it from bugs and keep it stored out of sight. To ensure your family's continued prosperity and abundance, place three antique or silver coins in a lucky red envelope at the bottom of the rice container. Change the envelope before each Chinese New Year.

Do use colors and light to create balance and har-mony in your kitchen.

DO

Do use closed bookcases, if possible, to keep the negative energy caused by the edges of the shelves from being directed at anyone in the room.

Don't use glass shelves in the N area. Don't place wooden shelves in SW and NE areas, or in the center of a room.

Do place inspirational literature, biographies about successful people, and personal growth and self-help books in the N area of a room or your home, which represents business and career success.

Do put college handbooks from a school of choice in the NE area to ensure academic success.

Do put reference and motivational books, cards, and posters in the NE area, which represents wisdom.

Do keep literature about starting or developing new ventures, businesses, or beginnings in the E, which represents spring and new growth.

Do put books about building wealth, making investments, and increasing your assets in the SE, which represents wealth, material growth, and fortune.

Do store gifts, books, pictures, and other items about and from celebrities in the S, which represents fame and fortune.

Do keep literature about international relations, trade, travel, leadership, organization, and planning in the NW.

Do place your library or study in the NE of your home, the area that governs knowledge, wisdom, self-improvement, and enlightenment. If you are fortunate enough to have walls with shelves, arrange your books according to the subject, once again matching them with their corresponding areas.

Do encourage your children to study in the library if their own rooms do not have a suitable NE corner.

Do put an aquarium or fish tank in your library.

Do use your library for enriching, cultural activities, such as listening to music, meditating, reading, or practicing a musical instrument.

Do store your books with their spines flush with the edges of the bookshelf in order to eliminate *sha* energy. A better solution is to use cabinets that have doors on them.

Do display fresh or silk peonies in your library, but not elsewhere in the house, if you are a married couple.

Do position Chinese lions correctly. The male with the ball under his paw should be on the left side as you face out of the building. The female with her lion cub under her paw should be on the right. The male lion represents the domain of the world at large; the female lion represents offspring and home.

303

LIONS

Do place lions in pairs outside
your home for protection. They
should flank the door and face
away from the building. Choose
pairs that are in proportion to the
size of the building they grace.

Do use lions with great caution, as they will cause harm to the persons or businesses that they face. Safer substitutes include a pair of unicorns, elephants, horses, or *fu* dogs, which resemble the Pekinese dogs favored by emperors and represent good fortune.

Do use doorknockers with lion heads if the lion is part of your family's seal or coat of arms. These offer protection to your household.

Don't place lions anywhere but on the ground. They are animals of the earth and are not meant to be on roofs, gateposts, or pedestals. A good rule is to never place a lion's image higher than a lion would naturally climb.

DON'T

Do place a large or heavy piece of furniture in the S area of the living room to "anchor" your family when you move into a new home. When you want to sell the house or move away, remove the item.

Don't place all of your furniture against the walls, which accentuates the straight lines of a room and creates a boxy feel. Try arranging your furniture at 45-degree angles to the walls along with a rug for a fresh look.

Do place green or purple items, wooden objects or furniture, and objects in groups of four in the SE corner of the living room. This corner is among the most important prosperity areas in a home, and these placements can activate the wealth of the home's occupants.

Do have a budding composer or poet work in the N area of the living room. North is the direction of creativity and communication.

Do hang four family pictures in wooden frames in the SE area of your living room if you consider your family the treasure of your home. If you cherish your friends, place gifts from them or pictures of them in the SE area.

Do group your collections and souvenirs in multiples of four in the NW corner if travel is important in your life. The NW governs interests outside the home.

Do place geodes in the SW to enhance love, romance, and relationships.

Do add a gold, red, or pink crystal heart to your romance corner.

Do place heart-shaped candles and accessories crafted in earth materials, such as stone, tile, terra cotta, and clay, in the SW to activate love, romance, relationships, and marriage. Use yellow, pink, red, and white objects.

Do hang a crystal chandelier in the SW area of your home, especially if this area contains your living room, to attract love.

Do create a romance corner in the
SW area of your bedroom.
Include pictures or figures of
happy couples and surround
them with hearts, flowers, doves,
and lovebirds.

Do collect heart-shaped containers made of terra cotta, china, or porcelain, or take stones from the beach that are shaped like hearts. Place them in groups of two in your romance corner.

Do keep a representation of a bat in a SW area to encourage marital contentment. In China, bats symbolize happiness, good fortune, long life, and protection.

Do use a *bagua* mirror to deflect *sha* energy that originates from straight lines or unpleasant neighbors. The red wooden frame is shaped like an octagon with a round mirror at its center. It is bordered in green with gold symbols from the *I Ching,* a sacred Chinese text. Be careful how and where you use it!

Do use reflective aids primarily for protection and only as a last resort.

Don't use a mirror to harm someone.

Do hang octagonal *bagua* mirrors on the outside of your home, but never on the inside.

Do use a flat octagonal or round mirror to deflect *sha* energy from common sources, such as garbage cans, dumpsters, or barking dogs.

Do exercise great prudence and caution when using a convex mirror. It takes the images it receives and sends them out again, possibly harming someone. This strategy can also backfire, bringing you mishaps and misfortune.

Do use a concave mirror with a red plastic rim to absorb negative energy without sending it back out toward its source. These mirrors turn the images they capture upside down like a fun mirror at a carnival.

Don't position a mirror so that it cuts off any part of your reflected head. To do so is unlucky indeed!

Do carry a small compact with a mirror or a hand mirror for protection. These flat mirrors work quietly and unobtrusively but can still deflect *sha* energy when directed at its source.

Do use metal door-knockers with shiny or polished surfaces, silver platters or trays, and pewter plates in place of mirrors.

Do sit in the corner farthest from the entrance to the room to have a "command" position.

Don't sit in line with the door, as you will be in the path of negative energy.

DO

Do keep your back toward a corner or a wall for support. If a post protrudes from the corner or wall, correct it by covering it with a hanging plant's draping foliage.

Do sit with a tall building behind you to
provide the support
of a "mountain" if your
back is to a window.

Don't face away from the door if you are conducting business from home. Business will symbolically come to you through the door, so don't turn your back on it.

Don't arrange your workspace so that you look straight out into a corridor or see the stairs, storage rooms, closets, elevators, escalators, or toilets.

Do be aware of the sharp corners of book-shelves, tables, equipment, storage units, posts, or other objects directed toward you or any part of your body.

Do put your computer in the N or W area of your office to enhance your creativity. Place the computer in the SE if you use it to generate income.

Do place an aquarium or tabletop fountain in the E, N, or SE. A small aquarium with black or blue fish in the N area of your desk or office will activate your business and career success. Guppies or a single arrowana are ideal for an aquarium made of glass and metal.

Do place a safe, which is usually constructed of metal, in either W or NW, which both represent the metal element. The safe symbolizes the prosperity and financial security of a business.

Do have a good balance of yin and yang when decorating your workspace. Balance light and dark colors, soft and hard surfaces, and smooth and rough textures in your choice of window treatments, furniture, and flooring.

Don't have any mirrors in your office, as they can reflect negative energy from clients to other people in the room. You should always maintain control over the energy in your office.

Do treat the files in your office with respect. They represent your past, present, and future business.

Don't keep your files near the bathroom or on a wall that is shared with a bathroom.

Do keep your files off the floor, on higher shelves and bookcases, rather than under your desk or table. This is especially important for your stock certificates, investments, property deeds, and other important documents.

Do keep the cords to your office equipment well hidden. This eliminates clutter and allows for the free flow of *chi.*

Don't buy or use any furniture previously owned by someone who has gone out of business, gone bankrupt, been jailed, or been divorced, no matter what kind of great deal you think you're getting. In the long run, these items will bring you bad luck and *sha* energy, negating any savings you may have achieved.

Don't have a skylight in your office, as it provides a way for wealth to leak out of the room.

Do keep a bird or a fish as a pet. Both of these animals represent wealth.

Don't keep the ashes of a pet (or person!) inside your home or on your property. This represents death.

Do match the color of your pet to the color of the season in which you were born. Keep a red bird or fish if you were born in the summer. Select a green one if you were born in the spring. White pets are for those born in the autumn. Black is the color to choose if you were born in the winter.

348

Do keep your pets and their habitats in the rear of the house. Reserve the front of the house for people and positive *chi* to enter your home.

Do place photographs of great mountains, such as the Matterhorn, Mt. Fuji, Mt. McKinley, Mt. Whitney, and the Himalayas, or other prominent land features, including the Sahara and the Grand Canyon, in the earth areas of SW and NE.

Do place photographs of campfires, fireplaces, or erupting volcanoes in the S area, which represents fire.

PICTURES

Do hang photographs of metal sculptures and structures that you admire, such as Calder's mobiles, the Golden Gate Bridge, the Brooklyn Bridge, or the Eiffel Tower, in the metal areas of W and NW. You can have pictures of ships, but it's better if the Titanic and other ill-fated or shipwrecked vessels are not among them!

Do put water-only pictures, such as paintings of the sea or photographs of waterfalls, streams, and lakes, in the water area of N. If the picture contains elements made of wood, including trees, or earth, such as mountains and rocks, be sure that the water portion dominates.

Don't hang water scenes above your head in your bedroom, as this suggests you will be smothered or drowned.

Do hang a close-up photograph, illustration, or painting of a mountain or forest behind you if you sit in your office with your back to the wall. This will lend support to you and your business.

Don't put pictures of water behind your desk or place a picture of a river flowing directly toward you.

Do hang a picture of a tortoise swimming in water behind you. This animal represents business success and long life and has been kept in Chinese gardens and monasteries for centuries.

Do hang your diplomas, awards, kudos, trophies, and other accolades and commendations on the S wall of your home or office. This direction represents fame and fortune.

Do hang pictures of yourself with the rich and famous in S areas.

Don't hang pictures depicting war, battlefields, cemeteries, death, skulls, gloomy scenes, or people with sad faces.

Do activate the love, romance, relationship, and marriage area of your bedroom (SW) by hanging pictures of happy couples holding hands, kissing or embracing. The frames should be made of porcelain, terra cotta, or china.

DO

Do check the balance of yin and yang in your artwork. If you are a woman, are most of your paintings filled with female images? If you are a man, does most of your art reflect male interests? Substitute art that includes the opposite gender, especially if you are interested in romance or marriage.

Don't hang pictures of pouncing
or attacking animals, fierce birds,
and dead fauna in your home or
office, particularly if they are
depicted as maimed, dismem-
bered, bleeding, decapitated, or
killed by violent or brutal means.

Do use a jade plant in the wood areas of E and S. It makes a welcome addition to the interior or exterior of a home or business, as jade symbolizes wealth and good fortune.

Don't keep plants in your home
that have sharp, spiky leaves,
thorns, barbs, or needles, such as
cacti. All of these are a source of
tiny "poison" arrows directed at
the occupants of a room.

Don't place spiky or thorny plants close to your front entrance or flanking the path leading up to your house. Put these "hostile" plants on the perimeter of your property, some distance away from your house, to create a natural deterrent to intruders.

DON'T

Do plant roses. Although they have thorns, they also have a pleasant scent that neutralizes the *sha* energy.

Don't keep a snake as a pet or bring an image of a snake into your home. In feng shui, the snake is considered a noxious, treacherous, and wicked creature.

Don't injure, harm, or kill a snake that takes up residence in or around your house or property.

Do keep a shed snakeskin. This is believed to bring you riches.

368

Do avoid desks, offices, beds, bedrooms, and chairs that are facing stairs or under them. Energy flows straight down the stairs, representing a "killing" arrow aimed directly at the people below.

Don't have your stairs face a bathroom, since they will direct you toward the most noxious part of your home.

Don't have interior stairs that directly face your front door or exterior stairs that continue all the way to the curb. These represent your wealth pouring down and out of your home.

Don't place an altar or a cash box under the stairs, where energy will be pushing down on it. Instead, energy should be able to flow freely around those objects.

DON'T

Don't have your front door at the bottom of the stairs, as in the case of a basement apartment below street level. Negative energy flows and collects in lower spots, just like drainage water.

Do place a statue of a three-legged toad on the floor inside your house, facing into the room as if just entering. You can also put it in a cabinet, under chairs and furniture, or diagonally across from your front entrance. This toad symbolizes that money is on its way to you and is considered lucky.

Don't put a toad statue directly facing your front door or on an altar; this means that your money is on its way out the door.

Do keep a coin in the mouth of a toad statue.

Don't place toad statues in a bedroom, bathroom, or kitchen. They are thought to bring bad luck and negative energy when located in those rooms.

Do plant trees in a row or curving around your house, similar to arms embracing your home, to symbolize wealth and good luck.

Do plant lots of pine trees in the S part of your property. These trees symbolize longevity because they live for many years and contribute to good health by producing much oxygen.

Do keep all of the trees on your property topped and thinned out to allow the yang energy of the sun to penetrate through their branches. Trees can create a lot of yin energy because of their shade.

Do plant evergreen trees with broad or rounded leaves rather than pointed leaves.

Do plant two small trees to flank your entrance and act as guardians to your home.

Do stand in a pine grove or forest to do your exercises. This is believed to be the most healthful location for you.

Don't use the Hollywood juniper on your property. Juniper represents long life, but the Hollywood juniper resembles clawlike fingers.

Do plant prosperity bamboo in the E or SE to stimulate the aspects of life associated with those areas, including family, health, harmony, nutrition, prosperity, and abundance. It also makes a lovely gift to give to friends, relatives, and new businesses.

Don't plant a willow tree on your property or hold your marriage ceremony under one. Although graceful and lovely to look at, this tree is associated with sadness.

Do plant versions of the "money tree," such as jade, plumeria, ginkgo, poplar, and prosperity bamboo, in the SE or E section of your yard to activate your wealth.

Don't keep a potted tree in the center of your house. The center of the house is the earth element and represents harmonious relationships. Earth is destroyed by wood, symbolized by the tree.

Do plant trees in groups of three, six, or nine in your front yard, as these are auspicious yang numbers.

Do watch the shape of your trees. Don't have any that resemble animals or other creatures.

Don't have the trunk of a tree facing your front door. It will block your view of the world outside and will obstruct beneficial *chi*.

Don't cut down old trees, which are considered sacred and possess strong energy. However, if a tree is diseased or damaged by lightning, you may have to remove the dead branches or the entire tree. This is particularly critical if you have sick or elderly family members living in your home.

Do cover tree stumps with creep-
ing vines or ivy, or put large potted plants on top of them. A
dead stump emanates yin energy
and must be balanced by the
yang energy of a live plant.

Don't let the leaves of trees touch the building. The leaves represent the bones of the occupants of a house and will draw *chi* away from it.

Do keep a live turtle, especially if it is black, in N areas. Turtles are symbols of longevity, good luck, strength, fortune, and endurance. As one of the celestial animals, they are believed to possess great protective powers.

Do save a turtle by purchasing it from a market where it is being sold as food. This is especially meritorious because the turtle is considered sacred in China.

TURTLES

Do place crystal turtles facing N. Metal turtles should face W; wooden turtles should face E or SE. Turtles made of earth materials should face SW or NE.

Do use turtles, which represent long life, to rid your home of illness.

Do put a pair of Chinese unicorns on either side of your front entrance. They bring protection and attract fortune and good luck.

395

Don't allow the corner of a swimming pool with straight sides to point directly toward your house, especially toward a bedroom. The corner creates *sha* energy.

Do balance a water element on the left side of your front door (as you are looking out) with trees on the right.

Don't place water struc-
tures in your front yard
unless they face N,
which represents the
element of water.

DON'T

Don't put a pond or fountain near the right side of the door (as you are looking out), for it will encourage infidelity in your partner.

Do balance water, which is yin, with the yang energy of large boulders protruding from the water. Or allow sun or artificial light to reflect from the water's surface.

Do surround your water structure with the yang energy of color, sound, tiles, river stones, water plants or living creatures, such as fish.

Do have curving or slow-moving water in front of your house; this is considered auspicious. However, if the flow is rushing or is located behind your house, it will carry away your family's prosperity.

Don't have a pond surrounded and darkened by deep woods or dense trees. This is overwhelmingly yin and such imbalance is not good feng shui.

Do enhance an oyster-shaped pond with a focal point, such as a large stone, fountain, gazebo, or pavilion, where the pearl would have been.

DON'T

Don't put any fountains, ponds, or other water elements in front of your main entrance if it faces S, which represents the element of fire and symbolizes fame and fortune. Water destroys fire.

WOLVES

Don't place a statue of a wolf inside your home. The wolf symbolizes cruelty, greed, mistrust, and fear.

Do place a statue of a wolf as a guardian outside your home, perhaps in the garage.

Do use the animals of the Chinese zodiac as decoration in your home.

OTHER STOREY TITLES
YOU WILL ENJOY

The Feng Shui Garden: Design Your Garden for Health, Wealth, and Happiness, by Gill Hale. This highly accessible, practical book shows readers how to direct and make use of the natural flow of energy in a garden, patio, balcony, or backyard. 128 pages. Paperback. ISBN 1-58017-022-6.

Feng Shui: How to Create Harmony and Balance in Your Living and Working Environment, by Belinda Henwood and Howard Choy. This beginner-friendly guide features dozens of room designs to help readers maximize the flow of energy in their home or office, plus simple, inexpensive "cures" to positively influence relationships, careers, and more. 80 pages. Hardcover. ISBN 1-58017-170-2.

Feng Shui Tips for a Better Life, by David Daniel Kennedy. With this easy-to-use, easy-to-understand resource, even beginners can use the ancient Chinese art of feng shui to attract desired life changes in the areas of health, romance, career opportunities, and more. 176 pages. Paperback. ISBN 1-58017-038-2.

These and other Storey books are available at your bookstore, farm store, garden center, or directly from Storey Books, 210 MASS MoCA Way, North Adams, MA 01247, or by calling 800-441-5700. Or visit our Web site at www.storey.com.